Great Figures in Black History

BUFFALO SOLDIERS

Theia Lake

PowerKiDS press

Published in 2024 by The Rosen Publishing Group, Inc.
2544 Clinton Street, Buffalo, NY 14224

Portions of this work were originally authored by Christine Honders and published as Heroes of Black History: *Buffalo Soldiers.* All new material in this edition was authored by Theia Lake.

Editor: Theresa Emminizer
Book Design: Rachel Rising

Photo Credits: Cover, pp. 13, 23 Everett Collection/Shutterstock.com; pp. Cover, 1, 3-32 Wall to wall/Shutterstock.com; Cover, pp. 1, 3, 30, 31, 32 ReVelStockArt/Shutterstock.com; p. 5 Yingna Cai/Shutterstock.com; p. 7 https://commons.wikimedia.org/wiki/File:Abraham_Lincoln_MET_DT1652.jpg; p. 9 spatuletail/Shutterstock.com; p. 11 https://commons.wikimedia.org/wiki/File:Henry_flipper.jpg; p. 14 https://commons.wikimedia.org/wiki/File:24th_Infantry.jpg; p. 15 Matteo Omied/Alamy Stock Photo; p. 15 https://commons.wikimedia.org/wiki/File:1899UStroops.jpg; p. 17 https://commons.wikimedia.org/wiki/File:Captain_Charles_Young_(5ce98f67bbee496d995ea879ecce99e4).jpg; p. 18 Nadia Yong/Shutterstock.com; p. 19 U. S. National Park Service; p. 21 https://commons.wikimedia.org/wiki/File:Pancho_Villa_bandolier_crop.jpg; p. 25 EWY Media/Shutterstock.com; p. 26 https://commons.wikimedia.org/wiki/File:HarryTruman.jpg; p. 27 Mike McCarville/Shutterstock.com; p. 28 Bill Chizek/Shutterstock.com.

Library of Congress Cataloging-in-Publication Data

Names: Lake, Theia, author.
Title: Buffalo soldiers / Theia Lake.
Description: Buffalo, New York : PowerKids Press, [2024] | Series: Great figures in Black history | Includes bibliographical references and index.
Identifiers: LCCN 2023004523 (print) | LCCN 2023004524 (ebook) | ISBN 9781642826760 (library binding) | ISBN 9781642826753 (paperback) | ISBN 9781642826777 (ebook)
Subjects: LCSH: United States. Army--African American troops--History--Juvenile literature. | African American soldiers--History--Juvenile literature.
Classification: LCC E185.63 .L35 2024 (print) | LCC E185.63 (ebook) | DDC 355.0089/96073--dc23/eng/20230223
LC record available at https://lccn.loc.gov/2023004523
LC ebook record available at https://lccn.loc.gov/2023004524

Manufactured in the United States of America

CPSIA Compliance Information: Batch #CSPK24. For further information contact Rosen Publishing at 1-800-237-9932.

CONTENTS

BLACK SOLDIERS IN EARLY AMERICA

Long before slavery was **abolished** and Black people were recognized as citizens in the United States, they served as soldiers. Black soldiers fought in **regiments** in the American colonies. During the Revolutionary War (1775–1783), roughly 5,000 Black soldiers served the cause of independence. Some Black soldiers were free persons, but many were **enslaved**.

For the most part, the Continental army and states' **militia** were integrated, meaning that white and Black soldiers fought alongside one another. That would not be the case going forward.

Estabrook

Prince Estabrook was an enslaved man who served in the Lexington militia. Estabrook fought in the Battles of Lexington and Concord on April 19, 1775. He was wounded but went on to serve the revolutionary cause for the full length of the war. He lived through the war, gained freedom, and died in 1830 at around 90 years old.

Despite the **prejudice** they faced, Black soldiers served with bravery and honor. Black soldiers would later fight in **segregated** regiments. During the American Civil War (1861–865) they received the nickname "buffalo soldiers."

This stone in memory of Revolutionary War soldier Prince Estabrook's service stands in Lexington, Massachusetts.

AMERICAN CIVIL WAR SOLDIERS

In January 1863, during the Civil War, President Abraham Lincoln issued the Emancipation Proclamation. This order freed enslaved people in the Confederate, or southern, states. Though Black soldiers fought in the war before this point, the U.S. government began officially **recruiting** and training them. The first Black regiment was the First South Carolina Volunteers, a unit of freed enslaved people from Florida and South Carolina.

Black soldiers were paid less than white soldiers. They served in segregated units under the command of white officers. Still, by the end of the Civil War, nearly 180,000 Black men had served in the Union, or northern, army. About 19,000 Black sailors served in the Union navy.

The Female Buffalo Soldier

Women weren't allowed to fight in the army. However, many served as nurses, spies, and scouts. Cathay Williams was secretly the first Black female soldier. She used the name "William Cathay" and never told anyone she was a woman. She joined the army in 1866 and served as a buffalo soldier for two years.

"Slavery is founded in the selfishness of man's nature - opposition to it is [in] his love of justice."
—Abraham Lincoln

THE 1866 REGIMENTS

In July 1866, Congress put together six segregated regiments in the U.S. Army. They later became four all-Black regiments: the 9th and 10th **Cavalries** and the 24th and 25th **Infantries**. These were the first Black professional soldiers in a peacetime army. Some were formerly enslaved people and soldiers who had fought in the Civil War.

There are several stories about how these soldiers became known as buffalo soldiers. One reports that the American Plains Indians who fought the 10th Cavalry gave them this name because of their dark hair and strong way of fighting. The nickname came to be used to describe all Black regiments formed in 1866.

Why Serve?

Black regiments often were given failing equipment, or tools, and fewer weapons than they needed. They had older, slower horses and poor food. However, the buffalo soldiers had the lowest **desertion** rate in the U.S. Army. Why? Though paid less than white soldiers, the military wage and living conditions often were better than what was otherwise available to Black men at that time.

A mail stamp picturing a buffalo soldier on horseback.

SERVING OUT WEST

The U.S. government **enlisted** buffalo soldiers to control Native Americans living in the West. Many tribes fought against the government's plans to force them onto **reservations** while white Americans took over their historic lands. Buffalo soldiers fought in over 125 conflicts, or clashes, with Native American tribes, including the Cheyenne, Apache, and Sioux.

The 9th and 10th Cavalries were stationed in Texas between the 1870s and 1890s. They fought in several battles against the Apache as part of the American Indian Wars. In June 1870, buffalo soldier Sergeant Emanuel Stance became the first professional Black soldier to receive the Medal of Honor after leading his patrol in a clash against the Apache near Kickapoo Springs, Texas.

Building the West

Buffalo soldiers also were tasked with building **infrastructure** out West. They built forts, roads, and communication lines and mapped areas. They also were responsible for the safety of trains, stagecoaches, and the mail service and protected American settlers from outlaws and thieves.

Henry Ossian Flipper was born into slavery in 1856. In 1873, he was the first Black person to graduate from the U.S. Military Academy in West Point, New York. In 1878, Flipper became the first Black officer in the U.S. Army.

THE SPANISH-AMERICAN WAR

The Spanish-American War began on April 21, 1898. It lasted 10 weeks, ending on July 17, 1898. During that time, more than 3,000 Black soldiers went to Cuba to fight for the island nation's independence from Spain.

Buffalo soldiers took part in in the Battle of San Juan Hill on July 1, 1898. The 9th and 10th Cavalries and the 24th and 25th Infantries fought along with white regiments, making it the most integrated battle of the 19th century.

Lieutenant John J. Pershing was a white officer in the 10th Cavalry at the Battle of San Juan Hill. He later wrote of the buffalo soldiers, "They fought their way into the hearts of the American people."

Twenty-six buffalo soldiers died in the Battle of San Juan Hill.
Several were honored for their bravery.

THE PHILIPPINE-AMERICAN WAR

The peace agreement that ended the Spanish-American War gave the United States control of the Philippines. Some Filipinos called *insurrectos* wanted independence from Americans. Buffalo soldiers were sent to the Philippines in 1899 to fight them.

Many in the Black community thought it was unfair to send Black troops to fight this war when they didn't have equal rights in the United States. Some *insurrectos* even tried to persuade Black soldiers that they should abandon the United States. They gave flyers to the buffalo soldiers about how badly Black people were treated in the United States and promised they would be rewarded if they joined the Filipinos.

Many buffalo soldiers hoped that success in the Philippines would mean more respect at home.

AN IMPORTANT SOLDIER

Charles Young was born to enslaved parents on March 12, 1864. A year later, his father escaped to freedom and joined the Fifth Regiment, U.S. Colored Heavy Artillery. Young's family moved to Ripley, Ohio, where he was educated at an integrated school.

Young became the third Black person to graduate from the U.S. Military Academy at West Point, New York, and to be made an army officer. He served out West, in the Spanish-American War, and in the Philippines. By the end of Young's career, he had become a colonel, the highest rank a Black service member had ever received.

A Guard of Honor

In May 1903, Captain Young and his soldiers received an exciting task. They were made the "guard of honor" for President Theodore Roosevelt, leading him through the streets of San Francisco. This was the first time Black soldiers were given this honor.

Charles Young was also the first Black national park superintendent.

NATIONAL PARKS

Along with their military service, buffalo soldiers served as caretakers of the national parks. Soldiers were stationed at Yosemite and Sequoia National Parks. They were expected to fight fires, build roads, protect park wildlife, and more.

YOSEMITE

In 1903, Charles Young was made company commander of the Ninth Cavalry at the Presidio of San Francisco, California, a military post. He and his troops marched 323 miles (520 km) to Sequoia National Park. U.S. soldiers had been managing California's parks during the summers since 1891, but Black soldiers had never patrolled them before. Young and the Ninth Cavalry were responsible for protecting the forest and building infrastructure.

Buffalo soldiers were among the United States' first park rangers.

THE MEXICAN EXPEDITION

In 1916, Mexican revolutionary Pancho Villa led a force into New Mexico. Villa's forces attacked and killed citizens before fleeing back over the border. Brigadier General John J. Pershing led troops, including Charles Young and the 10th Cavalry, into Mexico to catch Villa. This was called the Mexican Punitive Expedition.

The 10th Cavalry fought in the Battle of Carrizal in June 1916. After this battle, the Mexican and U.S. governments began talks and U.S. forces soon withdrew from Mexico. The soldiers never caught Villa, but Mexican forces released 23 captured U.S. troops.

Pancho Villa is pictured in the painting to the left and in the photograph above.

WORLD WAR I

Despite the long history of the buffalo soldiers, when World War I started in 1914, Black Americans weren't allowed to enlist in the military. However, as the war dragged on, the government changed this rule as they needed the manpower of Black soldiers. Close to 368,000 Black Americans served in the U.S. military during World War I. Many were assigned to labor tasks such as digging ditches and building roads.

Despite the **discrimination** they faced, Black soldiers **distinguished** themselves through many feats of bravery. But no matter their victories overseas, the soldiers continued to suffer prejudice and mistreatment in their home country.

The Harlem Hellfighters

The 369th Infantry Regiment of the 93rd Division was an all-Black unit that trained under French command. They also were called the Harlem Hellfighters. The Hellfighters fought hard in France, suffering the loss of many soldiers. They were widely celebrated for their bravery and the French government awarded them medals. The U.S. government held a victory parade for the regiment in New York City in February 1919.

President Woodrow Wilson was openly racist. He claimed that Black Americans were inferior, or lesser, soldiers and leaders.

WORLD WAR II

While continuing to face mistreatment and discrimination, Black men and women served in every military branch during World War II (1939–1945). By the war's end, more than 900,000 Black Americans had served in the U.S. military. They worked and fought in segregated units, usually under the command of white officers.

As in previous wars, despite the prejudice they faced, Black soldiers distinguished themselves for their valor, or bravery. The Tuskegee Airmen were the first crew of Black American fighter pilots. During the war, they flew more than 180 **combat missions** without losing a single bomber.

The Fight for Civil Rights

During World War II, Black soldiers fought **fascism** overseas and racism at home. The Black men and women of the U.S. military offered their lives and service for the country, although they weren't recognized as equal citizens. The victories and contributions of Black American fighters and workers during the war fueled the fight for civil rights in the United States.

This is the Tuskegee Airmen National Historic site in Tuskegee, Alabama.

MILITARY INTEGRATION

In 1948, President Harry S. Truman passed Executive Order 9981. This order stated "that there shall be equality of treatment and opportunity for all persons in the armed services without regard to race, color, religion or national origin." It officially ended segregation in the military.

Although the order passed in 1948, it took some time to go into full effect. When the Korean War broke out in 1950, all-Black units were among the first sent into combat. During the Korean War, Black officers were able to lead integrated units and command white soldiers for the first time.

HARRY S. TRUMAN

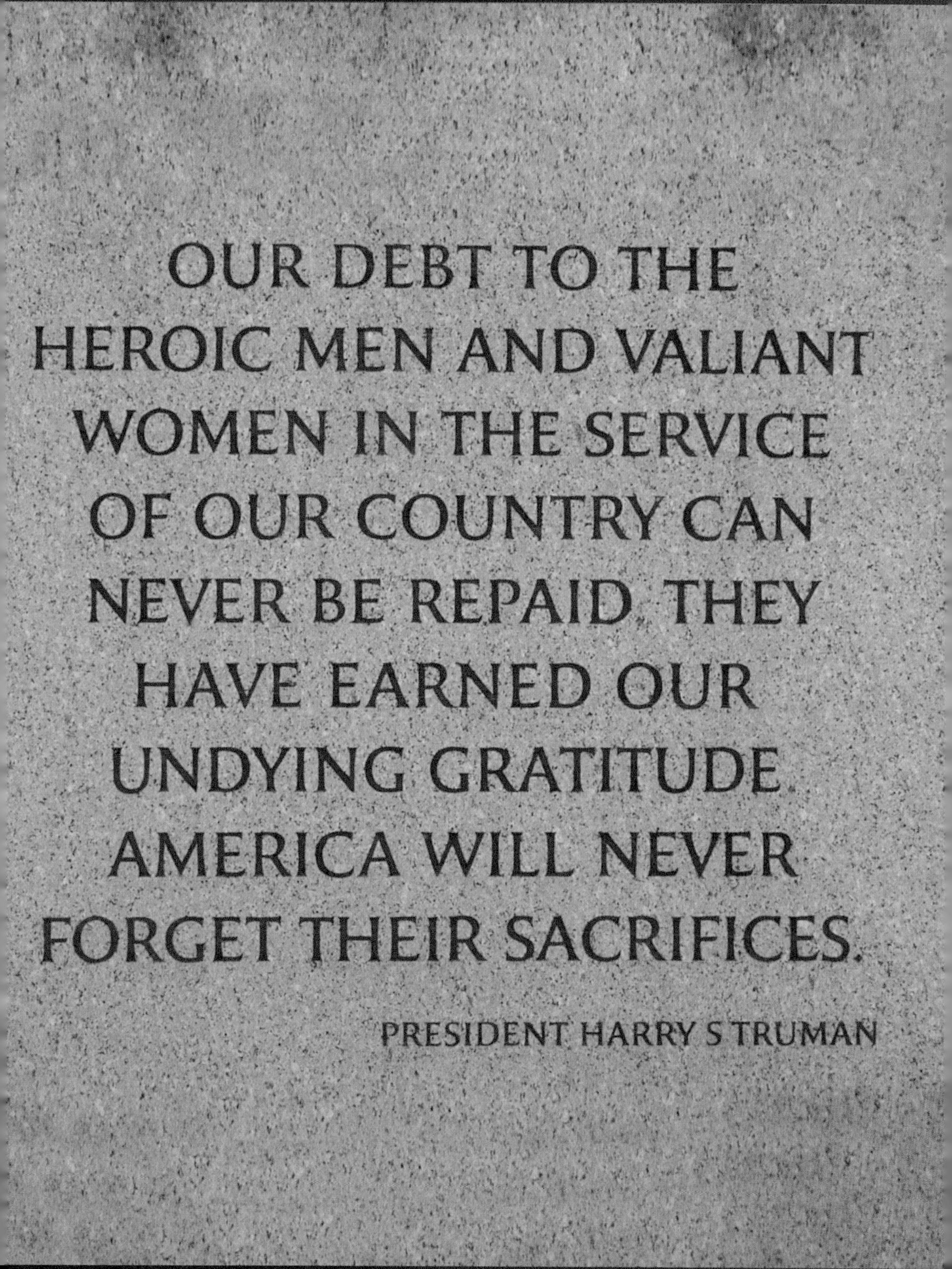
OUR DEBT TO THE
HEROIC MEN AND VALIANT
WOMEN IN THE SERVICE
OF OUR COUNTRY CAN
NEVER BE REPAID. THEY
HAVE EARNED OUR
UNDYING GRATITUDE.
AMERICA WILL NEVER
FORGET THEIR SACRIFICES.
PRESIDENT HARRY S TRUMAN

A LEGACY OF HONOR

For more than 200 years, Black Americans have served in every conflict in the nation's history, from the American Revolution to present day. Black American soldiers helped build, serve, and protect their nation while facing racism and discrimination within the military and at home.

Today, the U.S. military is racially integrated. The buffalo soldiers were leaders in the long road to legal racial equality, though it was accomplished long after their lives were over. Today we look back on the difficulties they faced, the sacrifices they made, and the service they offered, saluting the legacy of honor and courage they left behind.

TIMELINE OF THE BUFFALO SOLDIERS

1866

Congress creates six segregated army regiments of Black soldiers in the U.S. Army, which become four all-Black regiments.

1867

The buffalo soldiers are sent to the western frontier.

1870

Sergeant Emanuel Stance becomes the first Black soldier to receive the Medal of Honor.

1878

Henry O. Flipper becomes the first Black officer in the U.S. Army.

1898

Buffalo soldiers fight in the Battle of San Juan Hill in Cuba.

1899

Buffalo soldiers are sent to the Philippines to fight the insurrectos.

1903

Captain Charles Young and other buffalo soldiers escort President Theodore Roosevelt through San Francisco. They later march to Sequoia National Park.

1916

General John J. Pershing leads buffalo soldiers in the Mexican Punitive Expedition.

1944

The 9th and 10th Cavalries provide supplies and services to soldiers during World War II.

1948

President Harry Truman passes Executive Order 9981 ending military segregation.

1954

The last segregated units are disbanded.

GLOSSARY

abolish: To officially end or stop something, especially slavery.

cavalry: The part of an army made up of soldiers trained to fight on horseback.

combat mission: A fight or battle with a certain purpose or goal.

desertion: Leaving the military without permission.

discrimination: Unfair treatment based on factors such as a person's race, age, religion, or gender.

distinguish: To recognize one thing from others by some mark or quality.

enlist: To sign up or bring someone onto something for a purpose.

enslaved: Living in slavery.

fascism: A far-right form of government in which most of a country's power is held by one leader (such as Hitler's government during WWII).

infantry: The part of an army made up of soldiers trained to fight on foot.

infrastructure: The equipment and structures needed for a country, state, or region to function properly.

militia: A military force that is raised from civilians (nonmilitary citizens) to help out during a time of war or emergency.

prejudice: An unfair feeling of dislike for a person or group because of race or religious or political beliefs.

recruit: To get the services of someone.

regiment: A fighting unit.

reservation: Land set aside by the government for specific Native American tribes to live on.

segregated: Set apart or separated from others, especially because of race.

FOR MORE INFORMATION

Books

Idzikowski, Lisa. *The Real Story Behind the Civil War.* New York, NY: PowerKids Press, 2020.

Stoltman, Joan. *Did the Abolition Movement Abolish Slavery?* New York, NY: PowerKids Press, 2019.

Websites

Buffalo Soldiers National Museum

buffalosoldiersmuseum.org/the-buffalo-soldiers/

Learn more about the history of the buffalo soldiers.

National Park Service

www.nps.gov/subjects/buffalosoldiers/about.htm

Read about life as a buffalo soldier, learn the stories of individuals, and understand more about buffalo soldiers' service.

INDEX